EMERGENCY POEMS

Also by Nicanor Parra

Poems and Antipoems

Nicanor Parra

EMERGENCY POEMS

Translated by Miller Williams

A New Directions Book

Library of Congress Catalog Card Number: 71-181896

Some of these poems first appeared in *Atlantic Monthly* —and *Doors and Mirrors*, Carpentier and Brof, eds. Grossman, 1972.

Assistance for the translation of this volume was given by the Center for Inter-American Relations.

First published clothbound and as ND Paperbook 333 in 1972.

Published simultaneously in Canada by McClelland & Stewart, Ltd.

Manufactured in the United States of America.

New Directions Books are published for James Laughlin
by New Directions Publishing Corporation,
333 Sixth Avenue, New York 10014

INTRODUCTION

From the first publication of his work in English, Nicanor Parra has taught us—has forced us—to come to poetry with new eyes. More than that, he has made us look with new eyes at all the things of this world: airplanes and pencils, crankshafts and flies and pianos. He has redefined the poem in such a way as only a few have done. And in doing so he has redefined the world in which the poem is written and the hand that writes it. Aristotle was not more challenged by Hume, nor Aquinas by Calvin.

When Parra's lines seem disconnected, it is because they are connected in a supralogical way in which we are not accustomed to seeing things. When the conventions of cause-and-result seem to be outraged, they are.

The poetry has moved and expanded as the imagination behind it has since the publication of *Poems and Antipoems.* Those who are familiar with Parra's work will find the humor more sharply honed and darker, the anger closer to the surface and sometimes breaking through, the language tighter, the compassion deeper and the statements more political—or anyway more social.

Some of the satirical poems are as good as anything Parra has done, and those who recognize them for what they are will recognize also that taken on their own terms they stand with the best poems of social satire from any time.

Still, it would be a mistake to look inside these poems for confirmation of a reader's own political certitudes. Parra is not a pamphleteer; he is a poet. If he does seem to be a particular political animal in one line, he will turn around and bite the same animal in the next. What he does say consistently and clearly is that this is not the world we think it is, that we are walking on the edge of a precipice with our eyes closed. He says that we might open our eyes and see the precipice, where it is, and even each other.

It has been suggested in a recent essay that the antipoem, or whatever one decides to call what Parra writes, did not originate with Parra, since all of the elements—dark humor, disjointed logic, flatness of tone, directness of statement, suspicion of many of the stock poetical devices—were already in evidence in the work of one poet or another, one element here and one there, and that all Parra did was to bring them together. This seems a petty sort of pursuit, the throwing down of a glove in the back stacks of some library where graduate students might be arguing such points of literary history. Let it be enough to suggest here that what we usually call genius is the genius of assimilation, and that if this doesn't seem sensible, we had as well say that Edison did not invent the electric light, since all the elements—glass, metal, electricity—were all in use already, in one place or another.

Enough of that. What Nicanor Parra has given us is the poetry Nicanor Parra writes—and in this case, that poetry as I have translated it. Certainly all that I am saying depends upon the rightness of the translations. There is nothing to say to this except that the translations are here, and those who read both languages will know when the failure is great and when it is small. There is no success in translation. I have tried to be faithful both to Parra and to English, and to leave myself out of it as much as possible. I have tried to write what Parra would have written, if English were his language. We have been good friends for a long time; now and then I can get inside his mind. I have tried to stay there for the past few weeks.

Part of what is remarkable about Nicanor Parra's poetry is the sense it carries of the common, the everyday. We look at it and we almost say, "Hell, anybody could have written that; these are just simple statements." But we know that no one else could have written them—that's how simple they are.

Miller Williams

A special thanks to Patricio Lerzundi, a generous and patient man, who did much to make this book possible.—MW

EMERGENCY POEMS

ADVERTENCIAS

Se prohibe rezar, estornudar
Escupir, elogiar, arrodillarse
Venerar, aullar, expectorar.

En este recinto se prohibe dormir
Inocular, hablar, excomulgar
Armonizar, huir, interceptar.

Estrictamente se prohibe correr.

Se prohibe fumar y fornicar.

WARNINGS

No praying allowed, no sneezing.
No spitting, eulogizing, kneeling
Worshipping, howling, expectorating.

No sleeping permitted in this precinct
No inoculating, talking, excommunicating
Harmonizing, escaping, catching.

Running is absolutely forbidden.

No smoking. No fucking.

COMO LES IBA DICIENDO

número uno en todo
no ha habido no hay no habrá
sujeto de mayor potencia sexual que yo
una vez hice eyacular diecisiete veces consecutivas
a una empleada doméstica

yo soy el descubridor de Gabriela Mistral
antes de mí no se tenía idea de poesía
soy deportista: recorro los cien metros planos
en un abrir y cerrar de ojos

han de saber que yo introduje el cine sonoro en Chile
en cierto sentido podría decirse
que yo soy el primer obispo de este país
el primer fabricante de sombreros
el primer individuo que sospechó
la posibilidad de los vuelos espaciales

yo le dije al Che Guevara que Bolivia nó
le expliqué con lujo de detalles
y le advertí que arriesgaba su vida

de haberme hecho caso
no le hubiera ocurrido lo que le ocurrió
¿Recuerdan ustedes lo que le ocurrió al Ché Guevara
en Bolivia?
imbécil me decían en el colegio
pero yo era el primer alumno del curso
tal como ustedes me ven
joven-buenmozo-inteligente
genial diría yo
—irresistible—
con una berga de padre y señor mío
que las colegialas adivinan de lejos
a pesar de que yo trato de disimular al máximo.

AS I WAS SAYING

number one in everything
there has not been is not will not be
a man of greater sexual prowess than I
once I got a baby-sitter
to come seventeen consecutive times.

I am the discoverer of Gabriela Mistral
before me nobody knew what poetry was all about
I'm an athlete: I run the hundred meters
in the blink of an eye

as everyone knows I brought talking pictures to Chile
in a certain sense you could say
I'm the first bishop of this country
the first manufacturer of hats
the first person to see the possibility
of space travel

I told Che Guevara "Bolivia, No"
I laid it out for him in full detail
I warned him his life would be in danger

if he had listened to me
what happened to him would not have happened
remember what happened to Che Guevara
in Bolivia?
they used to call me an imbecile in college
but I was the best student in the class
I was just as you see me now
young—good looking—intelligent
a genius I would say
irresistible
with a dong long as a donkey's
schoolgirls can sense the size a block away
in spite of the fact I do my best to disguise it.

QUE HORA ES

Cuando el enfermo grave
Se recupera por algunos segundos
Y pregunta la hora a los deudos
—Reunidos como por arte de magia
Alrededor de su lecho de muerte—
En un tonito que hace poner los pelos de punta

Quiere decir que algo marcha mal
Quiere decir que algo marcha mal
Quiere decir que algo marcha mal.

WHAT TIME IS IT

When a gravely ill man
comes around for a few seconds
And asks his relatives what time it is
—Gathered as if by magic
Around the deathbed—
In a voice that sets their hair on end

It means something is wrong
It means something is wrong
It means something is wrong.

DISCURSO DEL BUEN LADRON

Acuérdate de mí cuando estés en tu reino
Nómbrame Presidente del Senado
Nómbrame Director del Presupuesto
Nómbrame Contralor General de la República.

Acuérdate de la corona de espinas
Hazme Cónsul de Chile en Estocolmo
Nómbrame Director de Ferrocarriles
Nómbrame Comandante en Jefe del Ejército.

Acepto cualquier cargo
Conservador de Bienes Raíces
Director General de Bibliotecas
Director de Correos y Telégrafos.

Jefe de Vialidad
Visitador de Parques y Jardines
Intendente de la Provincia de Ñuble.

Nómbrame Director del Zoológico.

Gloria al Padre
                    Gloria al Hijo
                                        Gloria al Espíritu Santo
Nómbrame Embajador en cualquier parte

Nómbrame Capitán del Colo-Colo
Nómbrame si te place
Presidente del Cuerpo de Bomberos.

Hazme Rector del Liceo de Ancud.

En el peor de los casos
Nómbrame Director del Cementerio.

THE DISCOURSE OF THE GOOD THIEF

Remember me when thou comest into thy Kingdom
Appoint me President of the Senate
Appoint me Director of the Budget
Appoint me Attorney General of the Republic.

Remember the crown of thorns
Make me Chilean Consul in Stockholm
Appoint me Superintendent of Railroads
Appoint me Commander-in-Chief of the Army.

I'll take anything at all
Administrator of Trustee Territories
Director General of Libraries
Head of the Telegraph and Postal Services.

Head of the Highway Department
Supervisor of Gardens and Parks
Governor of the Province of Ñuble. (1)

Put me in as Director of the Zoo.

Blessed be the Name of the Father
And of the Son
And of the Holy Spirit
Put me in as Ambassador to any place

Appoint me Captain of the Colo-Colo Team
Put me in if it pleases you
As President of the Fire-Fighters Union.

Make me Principal of the High School in Ancud. (2)

If it comes down to it
Put me in as Superintendent of Graveyards.

(1) Province where the poet was born.
(2) Small town in Chile's deep south.

INFLACION

Alza del pan origina nueva alza del pan
Alza de los arriendos
Provoca instantáneamente la duplicación de los cánones
Alza de las prendas de vestir
Origina alza de las prendas de vestir.
Inexorablemente
Giramos en un círculo vicioso.
Dentro de la jaula hay alimento.
Poco, pero hay.
Fuera de ella sólo se ven enormes extensiones de libertad.

INFLATION

Bread goes up so bread goes up again
Rents go up
This brings an instant doubling of all rents
The cost of clothes goes up
So the cost of clothes goes up again.
Inexorably
We're caught in a vicious circle.
In the cage there is food.
Not much, but there is food.
Outside are only great stretches of freedom.

LA SITUACION SE TORNA DELICADA

Basta mirar el sol
a través de un vidrio ahumado
para ver que la cosa va mal:
¿o les parece a ustedes que va bien?

Yo propongo volver
a los coches tirados por caballos
al avión a vapor
a los televisores de piedra.

Los antiguos tenían razón:
hay que volver a cocinar a leña.

THE SITUATION IS GETTING DELICATE

You only have to look at the sun
through a smoked glass
to know things are bad:
or maybe you think everything is fine.

I say we ought to go back
to cars pulled by horses
to steam-driven planes
to TV sets cut from stone.

The old folks were right:
We have to go back and cook with wood again.

LA CRUZ

Tarde o temprano llegaré sollozando
a los brazos abiertos de la cruz.

Más temprano que tarde caeré
de rodillas a los pies de la cruz.

Tengo que resistirme
para no desposarme con la cruz:
¿ven cómo ella me tiende los brazos?

No será hoy
　　　　　　mañana
　　　　　　　　　　ni pasado
mañana
　　　　pero será lo que tiene que ser.

Por ahora la cruz es un avión
una mujer con las piernas abiertas.

THE CROSS

Sooner or later I shall turn with tears
to the open arms of the cross.

Sooner than later I shall fall down
on my knees at the foot of the cross.

It's hard
not to marry the cross:
see how she holds me in her arms?

It will not be today
                tomorrow
                or the day after
tomorrow
            but it will be the way it has to be.

For now the cross is an airplane
a woman spreading her legs.

JUEGOS INFANTILES

I

Un niño detiene su vuelo en la torre de la catedral
y se pone a jugar con los punteros del reloj
se apoya sobre ellos impidiéndoles avanzar
y como por arte de magia los transeúntes quedan petrificados
en una actitud equis
con un pie en el aire
mirando hacia atrás como la estatua de Loth
encendiendo un cigarrillo etc., etc.
Luego toma los punteros y los hace girar a toda velocidad
los detiene en seco—los hace girar al revés
y los transeúntes electrizados corren—frenan bruscamente
retroceden a toda máquina
como en el cine mudo las imágenes se quedan en suspenso
trotan en dirección norte-sur
o caminan solemnemente a cámara lenta
en sentido contrario a los punteros del reloj.
Una pareja se casa—tiene hijos y se divorcia en fracciones de
segundo
los hijos también se casan-mueren.

Entretanto el niño
Dios o como quiera llamársele
Destino o simplemente Cronos se aburre como una ostra
y emprende el vuelo en dirección al Cementerio General.

II

Tal como se indicó en el poema anterior
el niño travieso llega al cementerio
hace saltar la tapa de los sepulcros
los difuntos se incorporan de las tumbas
se oyen golpes a la distancia
reina un desconcierto general.

CHILD'S PLAY

I

A child lands on the cathedral tower
starts playing with the hands on the clock
leans against them to make them stop moving
as if by magic the people passing are frozen
in the following position:
one foot in the air
looking backward like the pillar of Lot
lighting a cigarette, etc., etc.
Then he grabs the hands and spins them full speed
stops them dead—spins them the other way
and the people passing are jolted—brake abruptly
go backward lickety-split
like the images in a silent movie
they trot north to south
or move in slow motion solemnly
against the hands of the clock.
A couple get married—have children and get divorced
    in fractions of a second
the children get married too—die.

Meanwhile the child
God or whatever you want to call him
Destiny or just plain Chronos bored to death
takes off again flying toward the Public Cemetery.

II

As indicated in the preceding poem
the playful child takes off for the cemetery
breaks open the sepulchers
the dead rise from their graves
noises are heard in the distance
there is total confusion.

Los difuntos parecen cansados
con los pies llenos de tierra
y sin abandonar aún las tumbas
conversan animadamente entre sí
como deportistas que se dan una ducha.

Cambian impresiones sobre el Más Allá
algunos buscan objetos perdidos
otros se hunden hasta la rodilla en la tierra
mientras avanzan en dirección a la puerta del camposanto.

III
Muerto de risa el niño vuelve a la ciudad
hace parir monstruos
provoca temblores de tierra
desnudas corren mujeres con pelo
ancianos que parecen fetos ríen y fuman.

Estalla una tempestad eléctrica
que culmina con la aparición de una mujer crucificada.

The dead seem tired
their feet are covered with dirt
without even leaving their graves
they talk excitedly among themselves
like athletes in the shower.

They exchange impressions about the Land Beyond
some look for things they had lost
others buried to their knees in the earth
move toward the cemetery gate.

III

Laughing like crazy
the child goes back to the city
gives birth to monsters
creates earthquakes
hairy women run naked
old folks who look like fetuses laugh and smoke.

An electric storm strikes
coming to a climax in the shape of a crucified woman.

CARTAS DEL POETA QUE DUERME EN UNA SILLA

I

Digo las cosas tales como son
O lo sabemos todo de antemano
O no sabremos nunca absolutamente nada.

Lo único que nos está permitido
Es aprender a hablar correctamente.

II

Toda la noche sueño con mujeres
Unas se ríen ostensiblemente de mí
Otras me dan el golpe del conejo.
No me dejan en paz.
Están en guerra permanente conmigo.

Me levanto con cara de trueno.

De lo que se deduce que estoy loco
O por lo menos que estoy muerto de susto.

III

Cuesta bastante trabajo creer
En un dios que deja a sus creaturas
Abandonadas a su propia suerte
A merced de las olas de la vejez
Y de las enfermedades
Para no decir nada de la muerte.

IV

Soy de los que saludan las carrozas.

LETTERS FROM THE POET WHO SLEEPS IN A CHAIR

I

I tell it the way it is
Either we know everything beforehand
Or we never know anything.

The only thing they let us do
Is learn to speak correctly.

II

I dream of women all night
Some laugh in my face
Others give me rabbit punches
They won't leave me alone.
They're making war on me all the time.

I get up with a face like a thundercloud.

Which makes people think I'm crazy
Or anyway scared to death.

III

It's pretty hard work to believe
In a god that leaves his creatures
To their own devices
At the mercy of the waves of age
And all the infirmities
Not to mention death.

IV

I am one of those who greet the hearse.

V
Jóvenes
Escriban lo que quieran
En el estilo que les parezca mejor
Ha pasado demasiada sangre bajo los puentes
Para seguir creyendo—creo yo
Que sólo se puede seguir un camino:
En poesía se permite todo.

VI
Enfermedad
                    Decrepitud
                                        y Muerte
Danzan como doncellas inocentes
Alrededor del Lago de los Cisnes
Semi desnudas
                    ebrias
Con sus lascivos labios de coral.

VII
Queda de manifiesto
Que no hay habitantes en la luna

Que las sillas son mesas
Que las mariposas son flores en movimiento perpetuo
Que la verdad es un error colectivo

Que el espíritu muere con el cuerpo

Queda de manifiesto
Que las arrugas no son cicatrices.

V

Young poets
Write any way you want to
In whatever style you please
Too much blood has gone under the bridge
To go on believing—I believe—
That only one road is right:
In poetry everything is permitted.

VI

Infirmity
        Decrepitude
                and Death
Dance like innocent maidens
Around Swan Lake
Half-naked
        drunk
With their coral lascivious lips.

VII

It's clear enough
That there are no people on the moon

That chairs are tables
That butterflies are flowers in perpetual motion
That truth is a collective error

That the spirit dies with the body

It's clear enough
That wrinkles are not scars.

VIII

Cada vez que por una u otra razón
He debido bajar
De mi pequeña torre de tablas
He regresado tiritando de frío
De soledad
            de miedo
                        de dolor.

IX

Ya desaparecieron los tranvías
Han cortado los árboles
El horizonte se ve lleno de cruces.

Marx ha sido negado siete veces
Y nosotros todavía seguimos aquí.

X

Alimentar abejas con hiel
Inocular el semen por la boca
Arrodillarse en un charco de sangre
Estornudar en la capilla ardiente
Ordeñar una vaca
Y lanzarle su propia leche por la cabeza.

XI

De los nubarrones del desayuno
A los truenos de la hora de almuerzo
Y de ahí a los relámpagos de la comida.

VIII

Whenever for whatever reason
I've had to climb down
From my little wooden tower
I've drawn back shivering from the cold
From loneliness
                    from fear
                              from pain.

IX

The trolley tracks have all disappeared
They've cut down the trees
The horizon is filled with crosses.

Marx has been denied seven times
And we keep on keeping on.

X

Raise bees on bile
Inoculate semen into the mouth
Kneel in a puddle of blood
Sneeze in a funeral parlor.
Milk a cow
And throw the milk in its face

XI

From the thunderheads of breakfast
On to the thunder of noon
On to the lightning of supper.

XII

Yo no me pongo triste fácilmente
Para serles sincero
Hasta las calaveras me dan risa.
Los saluda con lágrimas de sangre
El poeta que duerme en una cruz.

XIII

El deber del poeta
Consiste en superar la página en blanco
Dudo que eso sea posible.

XIV

Sólo con la belleza me conformo
La fealdad me produce dolor.

XV

Ultima vez que repito lo mismo
Los gusanos son dioses
Las mariposas son flores en movimiento perpetuo
Dientes cariados
                    dientes quebradizos
Yo soy de la época del cine mudo.

Fornicar es un acto literario.

XVI

Aforismos chilenos:
Todas las colorinas tienen pecas
El teléfono sabe lo que dice
Nunca perdió más tiempo la tortuga
Que cuando tomó lecciones del águila.

XII
I don't get sad very easily
To tell you the truth
Even skulls make me laugh.
The poet asleep on the cross
Greets you with tears which are blood.

XIII
The poet's duty is this
To improve on the blank page
I doubt if it's possible.

XIV
I go along only with beauty
Ugliness hurts me.

XV
I say it for the last time
Maggots are gods
Butterflies are flowers in perpetual motion
Decayed teeth
easily broken
I belong to the days of the silent movie.

Fucking is a literary act.

XVI
Chilean aphorisms:
All redheads have freckles
The telephone knows what it says
The turtle never lost more time
Than when it stopped to learn speed from the eagle.

El autómovil es una silla de ruedas.

Y el viajero que mira para atrás
Corre el serio peligro
De que su sombra no quiera seguirlo.

XVII
Analizar es renunciar a sí mismo
Sólo se puede razonar en círculo
Sólo se ve lo que se quiere ver
Un nacimiento no resuelve nada
Reconozco que se me caen las lágrimas.
Un nacimiento no resuelve nada
Sólo la muerte dice la verdad
La poesía misma no convence.
Se nos enseña que el espacio no existe
Se nos enseña que el tiempo no existe
Pero de todos modos
La vejez es un hecho consumado.

Sea lo que la ciencia determine.

Me da sueño leer mis poesías
Y sin embargo fueron escritas con sangre.

The automobile is a wheelchair.

And the traveler who looks back
Runs the grave risk
That his shadow will not follow him.

XVII

To analyze is to renounce yourself
One can reason only in a circle
One sees only what one wants to see
Birth solves nothing
I admit I'm crying.

Birth solves nothing.
Only death tells the truth
Even poetry is not convincing

We are taught that space does not exist
We are taught that time does not exist
But just the same
Old age is a *fait accompli*.

Let science say what it will.

It makes me sleepy to read my poems
Even though they were written in blood.

¡SOCORRO!

No sé como he venido a parar aquí:

Yo corría feliz y contento
Con el sombrero en la mano derecha
Tras una mariposa fosforescente
Que me volvía loco de dicha

Cuando de pronto zas un tropezón
Y no sé qué pasó con el jardín
El panorama cambió totalmente:
Estoy sangrando por boca y narices.

Realmente no sé lo que pasó
Sálvenme de una vez
O dispárenme un tiro en la nuca.

HELP!

I don't know how I got here:

I was running along happy as you please
My hat in my right hand
Chasing a phosphorescent butterfly
Who drove me crazy with joy

And suddenly zap! I tripped
I don't know what's happened to the garden
The whole thing went to pieces
My nose and my mouth are bleeding.

Honestly I don't know what's going on
Either give me some help
Or a bullet in the head.

UN HOMBRE

La madre de un hombre está gravemente enferma
Parte en busca del médico
Llora
En la calle ve a su mujer acompañada de otro hombre
Van tomados de la mano
Los sigue a corta distancia
De árbol en árbol
Llora
Ahora se encuentra con un amigo de juventud
¡Años que no nos veíamos!
Pasan a un bar
Conversan, ríen
El hombre sale a orinar al patio
Ve una muchacha joven
Es de noche
Ella lava los platos
El hombre se acerca a la joven
La toma de la cintura
Bailan vals
Juntos salen a la calle
Ríen
Hay un accidente
La muchacha ha perdido el conocimiento
El hombre va a llamar por teléfono
Llora
Llega a una casa con luces
Pide teléfono
Alguien lo reconoce
Quédate a comer hombre
No
Donde está el teléfono
Come, hombre, come
Después te vas
Se sienta a comer
Bebe como un condenado
Ríe
Lo hacen recitar
Recita
Se queda dormido debajo de un escritorio.

A MAN

A man's mother is deathly ill
He goes for a doctor
He cries
On the way he sees his wife with another man
They are holding hands
He follows them at a little distance
From tree to tree
He cries
He sees a friend from his youth
We haven't seen one another in years!
They stop in a bar
They talk, they laugh
The man goes out to pee on the patio
He sees a young girl
It's nighttime
She's washing dishes
The man goes over to her
He grabs her waist
They waltz together
They leave together
They laugh
There's an accident
The girl is unconscious
The man goes to find a telephone
He cries
He comes to a house with lights on
He asks for a phone
Someone recognizes him
Stay for dinner man
No
Where's the telephone
Eat man eat
Then you can go
He sits down to eat
He drinks like mad
He laughs
They make him recite
He recites
He ends up under a desk asleep.

ESTO TIENE QUE SER UN CEMENTERIO

de lo contrario no se explicarían
esas casas sin puertas ni ventanas
esas interminable hileras de automóviles

y a juzgar por estas sombras fosforescentes
es probable que estemos en el infierno

debajo de esa cruz
estoy seguro que debe haber una iglesia

THIS HAS GOT TO BE A CEMETERY

otherwise there isn't any way to explain
those houses without windows or doors
those interminable lines of automobiles

and judging by the phosphorescent shadows
we're probably in hell

below that cross I'm sure
there has to be a church

EN VISTA Y CONSIDERANDO

YO Jehová decreto que se haga luz

en los tiempos modernos
los sacerdotes han abusado bastante
de las facilidades religiosas
—realmente no sé que pensar—
en un abrir y cerrar de ojos
se desentienden de sus deberes sagrados

otro tanto parece que sucede
con el resto de los seres humanos
en verdad—en verdad
hay una atmósfera tan espesa
que se podría cortar con cuchillo

es por eso que insisto en que se haga la luz

ustedes recordarán
que en la Biblia aparezco ordenando la mismo
—claro que desde otro punto de vista—
pero al revés de lo que rezan las S.S.E.E.
es un hecho que la luz no se hizo
o si se hizo alguien la apagó
—un demonio cualquiera—
alguien que no tenía idea de nada—
lo que no deja de ser divertido
ya que después de todo yo soy dios
y mis órdenes debieran cumplirse
(se me ocurre—no sé qué pensarán ustedes)

totalmente de acuerdo:
la Creación es un Acto Fallido
pero yo no voy a cruzarme de brazos
y como un organillero de barrio
repito mi vieja canción
a pesar de saber perfectamente
que los chilenos no creen en mí

AFTER DUE CONSIDERATION

I Jehovah decree let there be light

priests in modern
times have abused
the things of religion enough
—the truth is I don't know what to think—
in the blink of an eye
all the holy offices are ignored

the same thing seems to have happened
with the whole human race
verily verily
the air is so heavy
you could cut it with a knife

that's why I insist there has to be light

you'll remember
that in the Bible I do the same thing
—in another situation of course—
but just the reverse of what the scriptures say
the light didn't come
or if it did somebody put it out
—some demon or other—
someone who didn't know what was going on
it's something that never ceases to amuse me
well after all I'm God
my commands have to be obeyed
(or it seems to me—I don't know what you think)

I agree completely:
Creation is a Lost Cause
but I'm not going to sit here and fold my arms
and keep repeating my song
like a neighborhood organ-grinder
in spite of the fact that I know perfectly well
Chileans don't believe that I exist.

Otro punto que desearía aclarar:
es un error bastante difundido
pensar que la Creación duró siete días
—es para condenarse de la risa—
la Creación aún no termina:
la Creación está por empezar!

Y para terminar un pequeño consejo:
a los llamados Padres de la Iglesia
no conviene tomarlos muy en serio

Another point I want to make clear:
it's a misconception too often spread about
to believe the world was created in seven days
—I could die laughing over that one—
Creation is still not finished:
Creation is just beginning!

In closing, a word of advice:
those people called the fathers of the church
shouldn't be taken very seriously.

JUBILACION

A los primeros síntomas de primavera
Llegan los jubilados
A la Plaza de Armas de Santiago de Chile
Y se sientan en los escaños de fierro
Con una pierna arriba de la otra
A disfrutar del aire transparente
Bajo una lluvia de palomas grises.

Los jubilados viven en simbiosis
Con esas aves de color temblor:
Ellos las corroboran con maní
Y ellas
          a picotones amistosos
Les extraen la carne de las muelas.

Los jubilados son a las palomas
Lo que los cocodrilos a los ángeles.

FRASES

No nos echemos tierra a los ojos
El automóvil es una silla de ruedas
El león está hecho de corderos
Los poetas no tienen biografía
La muerte es un hábito colectivo
Los niños nacen para ser felices
La realidad tiende a desaparecer
Fornicar es un acto diabólico
Dios es un buen amigo de los pobres.

THE PENSIONERS

At the first hint of spring
The pensioners come
Into the Plaza de Armas in Santiago Chile
To sit on the iron benches
With one leg crossed over the other
To enjoy the transparent air
Under a deluge of gray pigeons.

The pensioners live in symbiosis
With these birds of trembling colors:
The old men make an offering of peanuts—
The birds
            with friendly pecks
Pick the old men's teeth.

The pensioners are to the pigeons
What crocodiles are to the angels.

SENTENCES

Let's not fool ourselves
The automobile is a wheelchair
A lion is made of lambs
Poets have no biographies
Death is a collective habit
Children are born to be happy
Reality has a tendency to fade away
Fucking is a diabolical act
God is a good friend of the poor

SARANGUACO

Es de noche, no piensa ser de noche
Es de día, no piensa ser de día.

Cómo va a ser de noche si es de día
Cómo va a ser de día si es de noche
¿Creen que están hablando con un loco?

Ojalá fuera realmente de día.

Hace frío pero yo tengo calor
Hace calor pero yo me muero de frío.

Dije que hacía frío pero miento
Hace un calor que derrite las piedras
Eso lo veo con mis propios ojos:
¡Falso! ¡No veo nada!
¡Tengo los ojos herméticamente cerrados!

Lo que sucede es que me siento mal
Ese dolor de estómago de siempre
La sensación de vértigo no cesa.

Cómo que mal: ¡me siento perfectamente!
¡En mi vida me he sentido mejor!
¡Ojalá me sintiera desdichado!

Observen bien y verán
Que estoy riéndome a carcajadas.

SARANGUACO*

It's night, it doesn't seem like night
It's day, it doesn't seem like day.

How can it be night if it's day
How can it be day if it's night.
Who do you think you're talking to, some nut?

God I wish it were really daytime.

It's cold but I'm hot
It's hot but I'm freezing to death.

I said it was cold but I lied
To tell the truth, even the rocks are melting
I can see that for myself:
False! I don't see anything!
My eyes are hermetically sealed!

The important thing is that I feel bad
That gnawing pain in my stomach
The vertigo that never goes away.

Bad, hell: I feel perfect!
I never felt better in my life!
I wish I felt miserable!

Look closely and you'll see
I'm laughing blood and tears.

* An Araucanian Indian word: hodgepodge.

VIEJOS VERDES—ANCIANOS MADUROS

Sólo de la cintura para abajo
Fablan los pobres viejos libidinosos
Expulsados del templo de Minerva
Por infracciones de orden erótico.

Nosotros somos otra clase de gente:

Nuestros poemas cantan las hazañas
De los héroes,
                no los devaneos
De Cupido en el lecho de Venus.

Ellos son viejos verdes
Nosotros somos ancianos maduros.

OLD SWINGERS—PROPER GENTLEMEN

Only from the waist down
Do they babble, the poor old lechers
Thrown out of Minerva's temple
For breaking rules of an erotic nature.

We come from another class of people:

Our poems sing of the exploits
Of heroes,
not of the sins
Of Cupid in Venus' bed.

Old swingers is what they are
We are elderly and proper gentlemen.

AGNUS DEI

Horizonte de tierra
                        astros de tierra
Lágrimas y sollozos reprimidos
Boca que escupe tierra
                        dientes blandos
Cuerpo que no es más que un saco de tierra
Tierra con tierra—tierra con lombrices.

Alma inmortal—espíritu de tierra.

Cordero de dios que lavas los pecados del mundo
Dime cuántas manzanas hay en el paraíso terrenal.

Cordero de dios que lavas los pecados del mundo
Hazme el favor de decirme la hora.

Cordero de dios que lavas los pecados del mundo
Dame tu lana para hacerme un sweater.

Cordero de dios que lavas los pecados del mundo
Déjanos fornicar tranquilamente:
No te inmiscuyas en ese momento sagrado.

SUPONGAMOS QUE ES HOMBRE PERFECTO

supongamos que fue crucificado
supongamos incluso que se levantó de la tumba
—todo eso me tiene sin cuidado—
lo que yo desearía aclarar
es el enigma del cepillo de dientes
hay que hacerlo aparecer como sea.

AGNUS DEI

Horizon of earth
                    planets of earth
Tears, sobs held back
The mouth spitting earth
                    soft teeth
The body nothing more than a bag of earth
Earth of earth—earth of worms.

Immortal spirit—spirit of earth.

Lamb of God that washes away the sins of the world
Tell me how many apples there are in The Garden.

Lamb of God that washes away the sins of the world
Be good enough to tell me what time it is.

Lamb of God that washes away the sins of the world
Give me a little wool to make myself a sweater..

Lamb of God that washes away the sins of the world
Let us fuck in peace:
Keep your nose out of our holy business.

WE LET IT GO THAT HE WAS A PERFECT MAN

we let it go that he was crucified
we even say that he arose from the dead
—no sweat about that—
what I'd like to get cleared away
is what happened to the toothbrush
somehow or other we have to find it.

REGLA DE TRES

Independientemente
De los veinte millones de desaparecidos
Cuánto creen ustedes que costó
La campaña de endiosamiento de Stalin
En dinero constante y sonante:

Porque los monumentos cuestan plata.

¿Cuánto creen ustedes que costó
Demoler esas masas de concreto?

Sólo la remoción de la momia
Del mausoleo a la fosa común
Ha debido costar una fortuna.

¿Y cuánto creen ustedes que gastaremos
En reponer esas estatuas sagradas?

THE RULE OF THREE

Not counting
The twenty million missing
How much do you think the deification of Stalin
Came to in cold, hard cash.

Monuments cost money.

What do you think it cost
To pull down those concrete hulks?

Simply moving the body
Out of the mausoleum to the common grave
Must have cost a fortune.

And what do you think we'll spend
Putting those sacred statues back in place?

CHILE

Da risa ver a los campesinos de Santiago de Chile
con el ceño fruncido
ir y venir por las calles del centro
o por las calles de los alrededores
preocupados-lívidos-muertos de susto
por razones de orden político
por razones de orden sexual
por razones de orden religioso
dando por descontada la existencia
de la ciudad y de sus habitantes:
aunque está demostrado que los habitantes aún no han nacido
ni nacerán antes de sucumbir
y Santiago de Chile es un desierto.

Creemos ser país
y la verdad es que somos apenas paisaje.

CHILE

It's fun to see the peasants of Santiago Chile
come and go along the downtown streets
or move along the streets on the outskirts of town
with puckered faces—pale—worried—frightened to death
about the political order
about the sexual order
about the religious order
taking for granted
that the city and its people exist:
even though it's been shown
that the people are not yet born
and won't be before they die
and Santiago Chile is a desert.

We think we're a country
the truth is we're barely a landscape.

SENORA

su niño está raquítico
déle jugo de carne
leche déle bisté con huevo
cámbiese inmediatamente de esta población callampa
cómprese un departamento frente al Parque Forestal
usted parece un espectro—señora
por qué no se pega un viajecito a Miami

PROPOSICIONES

estoy triste no tengo qué comer
el mundo no se preocupa de mí
no deberían existir los mendigos
que vengo sosteniendo lo mismo
años de años

yo propongo que en vez de mariposas
en los jardines anden cangrejos
—creo que sería mucho mejor—
¿imaginan un mundo sin mendigos?

yo propongo que todos nos hagamos católicos
o comunistas o lo que digan ustedes
es cuestión de cambiar una palabra por otra
yo propongo que purifiquemos el agua

con la autoridad que me confiere mi bastón de mendigo
yo propongo que el papa se deje bigote

estoy que me desmayo de hambre
yo propongo que me regalen un sandwich
y para terminar con la monotonía
propongo que el sol salga por el occidente.

LADY

your son has rickets
give him beef broth
milk give him steak and eggs
get out of this pigsty
get an apartment on Park Avenue
you look like a ghost, lady
why don't you take a little trip to Miami

PROPOSITIONS

I'm sad there's nothing to eat
the world doesn't give a damn about me
there shouldn't be any beggars
as I've been saying
year after year.

I propose that instead of butterflies
we put crabs in the gardens
—that would be better—
can you imagine a world without beggars?

I propose that we all become catholics
or communists or anything you say
it's a question of putting one word in the place of another
I propose we purify the water

by the authority vested in me by this beggar's staff
I propose that the pope grow a mustache

I am undone by hunger
I propose that somebody give me a sandwich
and then to have the monotony over with
I propose that the sun rise in the west.

SI EL PAPA NO ROMPE CON USA

si el Kremlin no rompe con USA
si Luxemburgo no rompe con USA
por qué demonio voy a romper yo

alguien podría tener la amabilidad de decirme
por qué demonios voy a romper yooo . . .!

SALTA A LA VISTA

que no debiera venir a los EE.UU.
—es comulgar con ruedas de carreta—
claro que por la misma razón
habría que romper relaciones con Francia
con Perú—con Bolivia—con Luxemburgo

no debiera moverme de Chile
pero quién engordaría con eso.

IF THE POPE DOESN'T BREAK WITH THE USA

if the Kremlin doesn't break with the USA
if Luxembourg doesn't break with the USA
why the hell am I supposed to do it

someone might be good enough to tell me
what the hell do you expect of meee . . .!

IT'S CRYSTAL CLEAR

that I shouldn't come to the U.S.
—I'm not about to buy that crap—
ok then for the same reason
we ought to break relations with France
with Peru—with Bolivia—with Luxembourg

I shouldn't ever set foot outside of Chile
but who'd get fat on that.

ENTONCES

no se extrañen
si me ven simultáneamente
en dos ciudades distintas

oyendo misa en una capilla del Kremlin
o comiéndome un hot-dog
en un aeropuerto de Nueva York

en ambos casos soy exactamente el mismo
aunque parezca absurdo soy el mismo.

VIVA STALIN

estos hijos de puta
no me dieron tiempo ni para ponerme el abrigo
sin decir agua va
me sacaron a punta de empellones
uno me dio un culatazo en el tórax
otro degenerado me escupió
pero yo no perdí la paciencia

me llevaron a una calle desmantelada
cerca de la estación de ferrocarril
en un furgón de los radiopatrullas
y me dijeron ahora puedes largarte

yo sabía perfectamente lo que eso quería decir

¡asesinos!
debiera haberles gritado
pero morí gritando Viva Stalin

WELL THEN

don't be confused
if you see me in two cities
at once

hearing mass in a chapel of the Kremlin
or eating a hot dog
in a New York airport

I'm the same person both places
although it seems absurd I'm the same person.

VIVA STALIN

those motherfuckers
wouldn't give me time to get my overcoat
with no warning at all
they grabbed me and knocked me around
one got me in the chest with his gun butt
another son of a bitch spat on me
but I never lost patience

then they took me in a patrol car
to an abandoned street
close to the railroad station
they said ok now you can go free

I knew exactly what they meant by that

murderers!
                    that's what I ought to have screamed
but I died screaming Viva Stalin

NO CREO EN LA VIA PACIFICA

no creo en la vía violenta
me gustaría creer
en algo—pero no creo
creer es creer en Dios
lo único que yo hago
es encogerme de hombros
perdónenme la franqueza
no creo ni en la Vía Láctea.

MOSCAS EN LA MIERDA

Al señor—al turista—al revolucionario
me gustaría hacerles una sola pregunta:
¿alguna vez vieron una flotilla de moscas
revolotear en torno a una plasta de mierda
aterrizar y trabajar en la mierda?
¿han visto moscas alguna vez en la mierda?

porque yo nací y me crié con las moscas
en una casa rodeada de mierda.

I DON'T BELIEVE IN THE PEACEFUL WAY

I don't believe in the violent way
I'd like to believe
in something—but I don't
to believe means to believe in God
all I can do is
shrug my shoulders
forgive me for being blunt
I don't even believe in the Milky Way.

FLIES ON SHIT

to this kind gentleman—to the tourist—to the revolutionary
I'd like to put one question:
have you ever seen a squadron of flies
racing around a pile of shit
come in for a landing and go to work on the shit?
have you seen flies some time or another on shit?

because I was born and raised with flies
in a house surrounded by shit.

FUERON EXACTAMENTE COMO FUERON

adoraron la luna—pero poco
fabricaban canastos de madera
no tuvieron idea de música
fornicaban de pie
enterraban a sus muertos de pie
fueron exactamente como fueron

ESTOS ENAMORADOS IDILICOS

se parecen como dos hormigas
como dos ojos de la misma cara
como dos hoyos de la misma nariz

estos enamorados putamadre
se parecen al mar en sus vaivenes
y se parecen al sol en sus manchas.

THEY WERE JUST THE WAY THEY WERE

they worshipped the moon—but not much
they made wooden baskets
they had no idea of music
they fucked standing up
they buried their dead standing up
they were just the way they were

THESE IDYLLIC LOVERS

could be two ants
two eyes in the same face
two nostrils in the same nose

these motherfucking lovers
could be the sea the way they go up and down
could be the sun if those were sun spots.

HABIA UNA VEZ UN MONJE

I

Había una vez un monje
que tenía muchos libros
sagrados y no sagrados.

Un día se le apareció
una muchacha desnuda
que parecía la Virgen.
Ella bailaba desnuda
arriba del escritorio
Y el pícaro se ayudaba
debajo del escritorio.

Había una vez un monje
que tenía muchos libros
sagrados y no sagrados.
Jamás se leyó ninguno.

II

Había una vez un monje
más lacho que el Padre Eterno
no le trabajaba a nadie
¡por qué voy a trabajar!
y se lo pasaba el día
sobándose la barriga.

Un día estaba rezando
detrás del confesionario
cuando apareció una vieja.
El monje se encabritó
y sin pensarlo dos veces
se desabrochó el marrueco
por ver lo que sucedía
¿y saben lo que pasó?
la vieja le dio un mordisco
que casi lo deja mocho.

THERE WAS ONCE A MONK

I

There was once a monk
who had a lot of sacred
and nonsacred books.

One day unto him there appeared
a naked girl
who looked like the Virgin.
She danced naked
on the top of his desk
the crafty scoundrel
helped himself under the desk.

There was once a monk
who had a lot of sacred
and nonsacred books.
He never read any of them.

II

There was once a monk
more lascivious than the Holy Father
he wouldn't go to work for anybody
Why should I work!?
He spent the days
massaging his belly.

One day he was saying his prayers
behind the confessional
when unto him there appeared an old lady.
The monk reared back
and without a second thought
unbuttoned his fly
to see what would happen.
Do you know what happened?
The old lady bit it so hard
she almost left him with nothing but a stump.

Al ruido vinieron todos
los monjes del monasterio
con velas y crucifijos
y al ver al monje sangrando
no pudieron contener
la risa los condenados.
El más barrigón de todos
decía empinando el cacho
fraile de los mil demonios
eso te pasó por lacho.

III
Había una vez un monje
más simple que un avestruz.

Un día lo sorprendieron
haciéndose la manuela
debajo del campanario.

Se le condenó a rezar
un credo y un Pater Noster.
Pero malhaya el efecto
que tuvo la penitencia:
la noche de Corpus Christi
un mocho lo sorprendió
detrás del confesionario
haciendo la misma gracia.

Fue condenado a rezar
un credo y dos Pater Noster.

He made such a noise
all the other monks in the monastery
came running with candles and crucifixes.
When they saw the bloody monk
the jolly beggars couldn't keep from laughing.
The most big-bellied of all
raising his horn said you have what you
deserve you fool of a thousand devils;
you see now what your sinful obsession got you.

III

There was once a monk
with half the wit of an ostrich.

He was caught one day
jacking off
in the base of the bell-tower.

He was ordered to say
a credo and a Pater Noster.
Fuck all the effect
the penance had:
the night of Corpus Christi
a lay brother caught him
celebrating the same rite
behind the confessional.

He was ordered to recite
a Credo and two Pater Nosters.

El vicio no se curaba:
un día que estaba absorto
arrodillado y en cruz
rezando un Ave María
se desabrochó el marrueco
y sin decir agua va
se puso a manyar la yuta
al pie del Altar Mayor
a vista de todo el mundo.

Los monjes se reunieron
a considerar el caso
y el más barrigón de todos
decía de cuando en cuando
fraile que nació chicharra
tiene que morir cantando.

There was nothing to cure the vice:
One day when he was totally absorbed
kneeling and crossing himself
saying a Hail Mary
he unbuttoned his fly
and without any warning
began to fiddle his diddle
at the foot of the altar
with the whole world watching.

The monks met together
to consider the case.
The most big-bellied of all
said this is a hopeless matter.
A bird is not going to sing
when it's born to chatter.

DESPIERTO AL AMANECER

excomulgado por los malos olores
y miro por el ojo tuerto del ventanuco:
una luna roñosa
deja caer sus gotas de sangre
sobre el jardín cubierto de nieve

en esto se oye la voz del contramaestre:
levántense carajo
ya debieran estar desayunados!

I WAKE UP AT DAWN

excommunicated for smelling bad
and look out the one-eyed turret
the blood of a scruffy moon
is dripping
into a snow-filled garden

and then the foreman's voice:
get up you dumb shits
you're supposed to be through with breakfast already!

TOTAL CERO

I

La muerte no respeta ni a los humoristas de buena ley
para ella todos los chistes son malos
a pesar de ser ella en persona
quien nos enseña el arte de reir
tomemos el caso de Aristófanes
arrodillado sobre sus propias rodillas
riéndose como un energúmeno en las propias barbas de la Parca:
en mi poder hubiese economizado vida tan preciosa
pero la Muerte que no respeta Fulanos
¿irá a respetar Sutanos Menganos o Perenganos?

II

Mientras escribo la palabra mientras
y los diarios anuncian el suicidio de Pablo de Rokha
vale decir el homicidio de Carlos Díaz Loyola
perpetrado por su propio hermano de leche
en Valladolid 106
—un balazo en la boca
con un Smith & Wesson calibre 44,
mientras escribo la palabra mientras
aunque parezca un poquito grandilocuente
pienso muerto de rabia
así pasa la gloria del mundo
sin pena
            sin gloria
                        sin mundo
sin un miserable sandwich de mortadela.

ABSOLUTE ZERO

I

Death doesn't even respect genuine humor.
for him every joke falls flat
even though it was Death
who taught us to laugh in the first place
take the case of Aristophanes
kneeling on his own knees
laughing like an energumen
in the very face of Death:
I would have spared that priceless life
if it had been up to me
but how is Death who doesn't respect Tom
going to respect Dick, Harry or Whatever-his-name-is?

II

While I write the word "while"
and the papers announce the suicide of Pablo de Rokha (1)
I may as well tell you about the murder of Carlos Díaz Loyola (2)
perpetrated by his own foster brother
at number 106 Valladolid
—a bullet in the mouth
from a Smith & Wesson .44,
while I write the word "while"
even though it seems somewhat grandiloquent
I say in bitter anger
thus passes the glory of the world
without pity
                    without glory
                                        without a world
without one miserable bologna sandwich.

III

Actuamos como ratas
en circunstancias de que somos dioses
bastaría con abrir un poco las alas
y pareceríamos seres humanos
pero preferimos andar a la rastra
—véase el caso del pobre Droguett—

Al parecer no tenemos remedio
Fuimos engendrados y paridos por tigres
Pero nos comportamos como gatos.

III

We act like rats
in spite of the fact that we're gods
spread our wings a little
and we'll look human
but we prefer to go on all fours
—take poor Droguett— (3)

We seem to have no choice
we were born of tigers by tigers
but we behave like ordinary cats.

(1) A Chilean poet/critic, remembered in part for his reference to the new Spanish poetry—specifically Neruda's *Canto General* and Parra's antipoems—as "pitiful and nauseating buffoonery."
(2) The real name of Pablo de Rokha.
(3) A socialist writer in Chile, not particularly friendly to Parra.

CUMPLO CON EL PATRIOTICO DEBER

de mirar lo que escupo
a lo mejor escupo un guarisapo
una vez escupí una catedral gótica
dos portaviones norteamericanos
tres autobuses armados en Chile
cuatro locomotoras a vapor
cinco globos aerostáticos
seis ataúdes con sus respectivos cadáveres
siete dragones que vomitan fuego
ocho o nueve carrozas funerarias
y una barbaridad de tomates podridos

COMO DICE MARCUSE

los estudiantes andan con el paso cambiado
hoy desvían un avión hacia Cuba
mañana asaltan un supermercado
—so pretexto de reunir fondos para la causa—
pasado mañana secuestran un diplomático
¡por qué no secuestran a la puta que los parió!

no se puede negar que por el momento dominan el escenario
pero la astucia vencerá a la fuerza
porque como les venía diciendo
los ancianos decrépitos férreamente unidos
haremos ver elefantes azules a los señores jóvenes iconoclastas.

I FULFILL MY PATRIOTIC DUTY

of looking at what I spit out
the chances are it's a tadpole
one time I spat out a gothic cathedral
two northamerican aircraft carriers
three buses assembled in Chile
four steam locomotives
five nineteenth-century aerostatic balloons
six caskets and their respective cadavers
seven dragons vomiting fire
eight or nine hearses
and a whole hell of a lot of rotten tomatoes

AS MARCUSE SAYS

students have their heads on backward
today they highjacked an airplane to Cuba
tomorrow they'll hold up a supermarket
—under the pretext of collecting money for the cause—
the day after that they'll kidnap a diplomat
why don't they kidnap the she-dog that whelped them all!

no one can say they don't have the stage for now
but cunning will overpower force
this is what I've been telling you
the old and worn-out welded into one
will make the young iconoclastic lords see blue elephants.

YO NO SOY UN ANCIANO SENTIMENTAL

una guagua me deja totalmente frío
no tomaría en brazos una guagua
aunque el mundo se estuviera viniendo abajo
que cada cual se rasque con sus uñas
aborrezco las fiestas de familia
prefiero que me peguen un garrotazo en la cabeza
a tener que jugar con un sobrino
tampoco me impresionan los nietos
es decir me ponen los nervios de punta
apenas me ven volver de la costa
se me tiran encima con los brazos abiertos
como si yo fuera el viejito pascuero
¡puta que los parió!
qué se habrán imaginado de mí

I'M NOT A SENTIMENTAL OLD MAN

a baby leaves me absolutely cold
I wouldn't take a baby in my arms
even if the world were caving in
every man scratches his own itch
I can't stand a family get-together
I'd rather be stuck in the eye with a sharp stick
than play with my nephews
my grandchildren don't move me very much either
what I mean is they set my nerves on edge
the second they see me come back from the coast
they come running at me with open arms
as if I were Santa Claus
little sons of bitches!
who the hell do they imagine I am

TELEGRAMAS

I
Déjense de pamplinas
Aquí no piensa haber gato encerrado.

Dios hizo el mundo en una semana
Pero yo lo destruyo en un momento.

II
Háblenme de mujeres desnudas
Háblenme de sacerdotes egipcios
A escupitajo limpio
Yo me arrodillo y beso la tierra
A la vez que me como un churrasco.

Yo no soy derechista ni izquierdista
Yo simplemente rompo los moldes.

III
¿Que para qué demonios escribo?
Para que me respeten y me quieran
Para cumplir con dios y con el diablo
Para dejar constancia de todo.

Para llorar y reir a la vez
En verdad en verdad
No sé para qué demonios escribo:
Supongamos qué escribo por envidia.

TELEGRAMS

I

Enough of this foolishness
Nothing is swept under the rug here.

God made the world in a week
I destroy it in a moment.

II

Enough of your naked women!
Enough Egyptian priests
Spitting all over the place
I kneel down and kiss the earth
With a hamburger in my mouth.

I'm neither leftist nor rightist
I just break the molds.

III

What the hell am I writing for?
I write to make you love and respect me
To satisfy God and the devil
To record everything.

To cry and laugh at the same time
Verily verily
I don't know what the hell I'm writing for.
I guess I do it out of envy.

IV
Como turista soy un fracaso completo
De sólo pensar en el Arco de Triunfo
Se me pone la carne de gallina.

Vengo de las Pirámides de Egipto.

En verdad en verdad
Las catedrales me dan en los cocos.

V
Sepa Moya quién hizo las estrellas
A lo mejor el sol es una mosca
A lo mejor el tiempo no transcurre
A lo mejor la tierra no se mueve.

Mientras esté en capilla
No moriré de muerte natural
A lo mejor las moscas son ángeles
A lo mejor la sangre de narices
Sirve para lustrarse los zapatos.

A lo mejor la carne está podrida.

VI
Con la llegada de la primavera
Dejo de ser un hombre del montón
Y me transformo en una especie de catapulta
Que proyecta gargajos sanguinolentos
Hacia los cuatro puntos cardinales.

Sólo la luna sabe quién soy yo.

IV

I'm a complete failure as a tourist
Just thinking of the Arch of Triumph
Gives me gooseflesh.

I come from the Pyramids of Egypt.

Verily verily
Cathedrals really grab me by the balls.

V

Heaven knows who made the stars
Maybe the sun's a fly
Perhaps time stands still
and the earth doesn't move.

It's crystal clear—
I won't die a natural death
Who knows? maybe flies are angels
Maybe nosebleeds are good
For shining shoes.

Could be the flesh is rotten.

VI

When spring comes
I'm no longer the man in the street
I turn into a kind of catapult
Flinging bloody phlegm
To the four points of the compass.

Only the moon knows who I am.

VII

Ha terminado el siglo XIX
Se me pone la carne de gallina.
Quién tuviera un dedo de frente
Para correr por los acantilados
Y pernoctar al pie de la vaca.
Miren esos magníficos zancudos
Esas insuperables obras maestras
Que se van desplazando por el aire
Como si fueran globos de colores.
¿Cierto que dan deseos
De tomar un pincel
Y pintarlo todo de blanco?

VIII

A propósito de escopeta
Les recuerdo que el alma es inmortal.
El espíritu muere
el cuerpo no.

Desde el punto de vista del oido
Luz y materia son la misma cosa
Ambas se sientan a la misma cama
Ambas se acuestan en idéntica mesa.

Entre ustedes y yo:
El espíritu muere con la muerte.

VII

The nineteenth century is gone
I get gooseflesh
I wish I had all my marbles
So I could run up cliffs
Sleep at the feet of a cow
Look at those magnificent mosquitoes
Those unfathomable masterpieces.
Floating in the air
As if they were colored balloons.
Don't they make you want to get a brush
And paint it all white?

VIII

Speaking of shotguns
I remind you that the soul is immortal
The spirit dies.
The body, no.

From the point of view of the ear
Matter and light are the same thing
They sit on the same bed
They lie on a single table.

Just between us:
The spirit dies with death.

TIEMPOS MODERNOS

Atravesamos unos tiempos calamitosos
imposible hablar sin incurrir en delito de contradicción
imposible callar sin hacerse cómplice del Pentágono.
Se sabe perfectamente que no hay alternativa posible
todos los caminos conducen a Cuba
pero el aire está sucio
y respirar es un acto fallido.
El enemigo dice
es el país el que tiene la culpa
como si los países fueran hombres.
Nubes malditas revolotean en torno a volcanes malditos
embarcaciones malditas emprenden expediciones malditas
árboles malditos se deshacen en pájaros malditos:
todo contaminado de antemano.

MODERN TIMES

These are calamitous times we're living through
you can't speak without committing a contradiction
or keep quiet without complicity with the Pentagon.
Everyone knows there's no alternative possible
all roads lead to Cuba
but the air is dirty
breathing is a futile act.
The enemy says
the country is to blame
as if countries were men.
Accursed clouds circle accursed volcanoes
accursed embarkations launch accursed expeditions
accursed trees crumble on accursed birds:
it was all polluted to begin with.

PREGUNTAS Y RESPUESTAS

¿qué te parece valdrá
la pena matar a dios
a ver si se arregla el mundo?

—claro que vale la pena

—¿valdrá la pena jugarse
la vida por una idea
que puede resultar falsa?

—claro que vale la pena

—¿pregunto yo si valdrá
la pena comer centolla
valdrá la pena criar
hijos que se volverán
en contra de sus mayores?

—es evidente que sí
que nó, que vale la pena

—pregunto yo si valdrá
la pena poner un disco
la pena leer un árbol
la pena plantar un libro
si todo se desvanece
si nada perdurará

—tal vez no valga la pena

—no llores

—estoy riendo

—no nazcas

—estoy muriendo.

QUESTIONS AND ANSWERS

do you believe it would be worth the trouble
to kill god
to see if that would straighten out the world?

—of course it would be

would it be worth the trouble
to risk your life
for an idea that might be false?

—of course it would be

I ask you now if it would be
worth the trouble to eat crab meat
worth the trouble to raise children
who will turn against
their elders?

—obviously yes
no, it's worth the trouble

I ask you now if it would be worth
the trouble to play a record
the trouble to read a tree
the trouble to plant a book
if everything disappears
if nothing lasts?

—maybe it wouldn't be

don't cry

—I'm laughing

don't get born

—I'm dying.

PASATIEMPOS

hacer brotar un mundo de la nada
pero no por razones de peso
por fregar solamente—por joder

desafinarle la guitarra al padre
masturbarse con pétalos de rosa
tonsurar a los hermanos menores
escribir aforismos en las murallas

asaltar a un anciano decrépito
discutir con los Doctores de la Ley
dispararle pelotillas al sacerdote
durante el desarrollo de la misa solemne
simular un ataque epiléptico
mientras alza la hostia consagrada
hacerse el cucho en un accidente del tráfico

espectorar en la capilla ardiente

acariciar un gatito romano
abrocharse y desabrocharse el marrueco
—si les parece me lo vuelvo a desabrochar

demoler el Hospicio
postergar indefinidamente la noche de bodas

seguir un curso por correspondencia
crucificar a Cristo Jesús
contraer una Enfermedad Venérea
someterse a un Examen de Orina
operarse de Cáncer a los Riñones
agobiar a los Padres de la Iglesia
con preguntas que no vienen al caso

PASTIMES

having a world spring from nothing
for no good reason
just to be a nuisance—just for the hell of it

getting your father's guitar out of tune
masturbating with rose petals
fleecing your younger brothers
writing aphorisms on the walls

mugging a decrepit old man
arguing with Doctors-at-Law
throwing spitballs at a priest
during the celebration of the mass
pretending to have an epileptic seizure
during the consecration of the host
playing dumb at a traffic accident

spitting on the floor of a funeral parlor

fondling a Persian cat
zipping and unzipping your fly
—if you want me to I'll unzip it again

tearing down an Old Folks' Home
putting off the wedding night time after time

taking a course by correspondence
crucifying Christ Jesus
contracting Venereal Disease
submitting to a Urine Test
undergoing surgery for Cancer of the Kidneys
wearing down the Fathers of the Church
with pointless questions

cocinar un sombrero de cura
a vista y paciencia de la Santa Sede

pronunciar un discurso patriótico
pero no por razones de peso
por fregar—solamente por joder
Señoras y Señores aunque no vengo preparado...

masacrar a quemarropa a la familia del Zar
incendiar la Biblioteca de Alejandría
descuartizar mujeres embarazadas
al más puro estilo Lyndon B. Nixon

en una palabra cagarse en el piano.

cooking a padre's hat
eyeball to eyeball with the Holy See

delivering a patriotic address
for no good reason
just to be a nuisance—just for the hell of it
Ladies and gentlemen unprepared as I am...

gunning down the Czar's family—point blank
burning the Library at Alexandria
drawing and quartering pregnant women
in the purest Lyndon B. Nixon style.

or in a word shitting on the piano.

JARDIN ZOOLOGICO

Dentro de algunos años sucederá lo siguiente:
Un elefante de dos tres metros de altura pensará para sí:
Yo soy un elefante útil a mí mismo
Mis pantalones respiran felicidad hasta por el marrueco.
Cuesta un poco andar hacia atrás—hacia lo alto
Hacia la imagen de otro elefante más bello que yo
Con el objeto de sufrir un pequeño cargo de conciencia.
Qué sería de un pobre elefante si le arrancáramos los colmillos
Y después le diéramos de golpes en las costillas
Hasta que dejara de existir.

A lo que la mosca responderá:
Hermano elefante, tus palabras nos desconciertan
Mírame a mí rebosante de salud
Marchar entre las hojas entre las flores
Entre las patas de los elefantes
Marchar en busca de otra mosca igual a mí.
Sigue el ejemplo de una mosca que piensa que sueña que sonríe
Y que generalmente hace su nido
En los yacimientos de abonos artificiales.

Este breve diálogo se llevará a efecto dentro de varios años
En un jardín particular dotado de luz eléctrica
En cuya puerta podrá leerse la siguiente inscripción:
"Jardín particular, viernes y sábado de once a doce"
Entonces el elefante despertará de su sueño infernal
Y apoyado en una especie de ataúd exclamará:
Dios protege a los animales.

THE ZOO

In the next few years the following things will happen:
An elephant twelve yards high will think to himself:
I am an elephant of some use to myself
My pants breathe happiness all the way to my zipper
It's not too easy running backward to high ground
Toward the image of an elephant more lovely than I am
So I can feel these small pangs of conscience.
What would a poor elephant be if we took out his tusks
And kicked him in the ribs
Until nothing was left.

To which the fly will answer:
What you say disturbs us, brother elephant
Look at me how I radiate health
Moving among the leaves among the flowers
Between the legs of elephants
Hunting a fly like me.
Follow the example of the fly who thinks who sleeps who smiles
Who generally makes his bed
In a pile of artificial fertilizer.

This brief exchange will take place over a period of years
In a private zoo wired for electric lights
On the gate of which will be read the following inscription:
"Private Zoo, Fridays and Saturdays, 11 to 12"
Then the elephant will wake up from his infernal sleep
And sort of leaning on a coffin will say
God takes care of animals

El no permitirá que yo muera
Las moscas suelen creerse perfectas
Ellas vuelan, a veces ellas van de un punto a otro
Mueven sus brazos y piernas a un mismo tiempo.
A lo que la mosca agregará:
Cordero de Dios, estos elefantes se están volviendo locos
Llenan de agua sus trompas que luego lanzan fuera de sí
Ellos corren a velocidades fantásticas
Por esos jardines particulares sin puertas sin ventanas
Como elefantes enfermos llamados a desaparecer.

En este momento sucederá lo siguiente:
La mosca crecerán hasta adquirir el volumen de un elefante
Y por su parte los elefantes bajarán de peso
Sus imágenes se reducirán una y mil veces
Hasta transformarse en pequeños elefantes de cocina de salón
Ellos serán unos seres diminutos que andarán por todas partes
En las frutas en el azúcar en la sopa
Y las moscas provistas de fuertes colmillos
Se replegarán hacia el extremo oriente.

He isn't going to let me die
Flies are accustomed to considering themselves perfect
They fly, sometimes they go from one place to another
moving arms and legs at the same time.
To which the fly will say:
Lamb of God, these elephants are driving themselves crazy
Filling their trunks with water and squirting it out
Running at fantastic speeds
Through those private zoos without doors or windows
Like diseased elephants doomed to extinction.

At this moment the following thing will happen:
The fly will grow suddenly to the size of an elephant
The elephants for their part will lose weight
Will shrink a thousandfold
They will become little kitchen elephants, parlor elephants
Tiny creatures running everywhere
In the fruit in the sugar in the soup
And flies armed with strong tusks
Will withdraw to the far east.

SIEGMUND FREUD

Pájaro con las plumas en la boca
Ya no se puede más con el psiquiatra:
Todo lo relaciona con el sexo.

En las obras de Freud es donde vienen
Las afirmaciones más peregrinas.

Según este señor
Los objetos de forma triangular
—Plumas fuente, pistolas, arcabuces,
Lápices, cañerías, guaripolas—
Representan el sexo masculino;
Los objetos de forma circular
Representan el sexo femenino.

Pero el psiquiatra va más adelante:
No solamente conos y cilindros
Casi todos los cuerpos geométricos
Son para él instrumentos sexuales
A saber las Pirámides de Egipto.

Pero la cosa no termina ahí
Nuestro héroe va mucho más lejos:
Donde nosotros vemos artefactos
Vemos, digamos, lámparas o mesas
El psiquiatra ve penes y vaginas.

Analicemos un caso concreto:
Un neurópata va por una calle
De repente da vuelta la cabeza
Porque algo le llama la atención
—Un abedul, un pantalón a rayas
Un objeto que pasa por el aire—
En la nomenclatura del psiquiatra
Eso quiere decir
Que la vida sexual de su cliente
Anda como las reverendas huifas.

SIGMUND FREUD

Bird with a mouthful of feathers!
Who can bear psychiatrists anymore?
They relate everything to sex.

The most astounding claims
Are found in Freud's works.

According to this gentleman
All tapered objects
—Fountain pens, pistols, blunderbusses,
Pencils, water pipes, dumbbells—
Symbolize the masculine sex;
All circular objects
Symbolize the feminine sex.

But psychiatry goes even further:
Not only cones and cylinders
Almost all geometric figures
Symbolize sexual equipment
The Pyramids of Egypt for example.

But that's not all
Our hero goes further than this:
When we see artifacts
We see, let's say, lamps or tables
The psychiatrist sees penises and vaginas.

Let's analyze a concrete case:
A neuropath is going down the street
All of a sudden he turns his head
Something attracts his attention
—A birch tree, a pair of striped trousers
Some object flying through the air—
In the nomenclature of psychiatry
This is to say
The sex life of the patient
Is in a hell of a mess.

Vemos un automóvil
Un automóvil es un símbolo fálico
Vemos un edificio en construcción
Un edificio es un símbolo fálico
Nos invitan a andar en bicicleta
La bicicleta es un símbolo fálico
Vamos a rematar al cementerio
El cementerio es un símbolo fálico
Vemos un mausoleo
Un mausoleo es un símbolo fálico

Vemos un dios clavado en una cruz
Un crucifijo es un símbolo fálico
Nos compramos un mapa de Argentina
Para estudiar el problema de límites
Toda Argentina es un símbolo fálico
Nos invitan a China Popular
Mao Tse-tung es un símbolo fálico.
Para normalizar la situación
Hay que dormir una noche en Moscú
El pasaporte es un símbolo fálico
La Plaza Roja es un símbolo fálico.

El avión echa fuego por la boca.

Nos comemos un pan con mantequilla
La mantequilla es un símbolo fálico
Descansamos un rato en un jardín
La mariposa es un símbolo fálico
El telescopio es un símbolo fálico
La mamadera es un símbolo fálico

En capítulo aparte
Vienen las alusiones a la vulva.
Vamos a silenciarlas por decoro
Cuando no la comparan con un búho
Que representa la sabiduría
La comparan con sapos o con ranas.

We see a car
A car is a phallic symbol
We see a building going up
A building is a phallic symbol
We are invited to go bicycle riding
The bicycle is a phallic symbol
We go by chance to a graveyard
The graveyard is a phallic symbol
We see a mausoleum
A mausoleum is a phallic symbol.

We see a god nailed to a cross
A crucifix is a phallic symbol
We buy a map of Argentina
To study the border problem
All of Argentina is a phallic symbol
We are invited to People's China
Mao Tse-tung is a phallic symbol
To normalize the situation
We have to spend a night in Moscow
The passport is a phallic symbol
Red Square is a phallic symbol.

The plane spurts fire out of its mouth.

We eat bread and butter
Butter is a phallic symbol
We rest a while in a garden
The butterfly is a phallic symbol
The telescope is a phallic symbol
The baby bottle is a phallic symbol.

In a separate chapter
We find the allusions to the vulva
Decorum prevents us from talking about that
When the comparison is not to an owl
Which stands for wisdom
The comparison is always to toads or to frogs.

En el aeropuerto de Pekín
Hace un calor de los diez mil demonios
Nos esperan con flores y refrescos.
Desde que tengo uso de razón
No había visto flores tan hermosas.
Desde que el mundo es mundo
No había visto gente tan amable
Desde que los planetas son planetas
No había visto gente tan alegre.

Desde que fui lanzado
Fuera del paraíso terrenal.

Pero volvamos a nuestro poema.

Aunque parezca raro
El psiquiatra tenía la razón
En el momento de pasar un túnel
El artista comienza a delirar.
Para empezar lo llevan a una fábrica
Es ahí donde empieza la locura.

Síntoma principal:
Todo lo relaciona con el acto
Ya no distingue la luna del sol
Todo lo relaciona con el acto
Los pistones son órganos sexuales
Los cilindros son órganos sexuales
Las tornamesas órganos sexuales.
Las manivelas órganos sexuales,
Los altos hornos órganos sexuales
Tuercas y pernos órganos sexuales
Locomotoras órganos sexuales
Embarcaciones órganos sexuales.

El laberinto no tiene salida.

El Occidente es una gran pirámide
Que termina y empieza en un psiquiatra:
La pirámide está por derrumbarse.

In the airport at Peking
It's hotter than ten thousand demons
They are waiting for us with flowers and refreshments
Since reaching the age of reason
I had never seen such beautiful flowers
Since the world was a world
I had never seen such friendly people
Since the planet was a planet
I had never seen such happy people.

Not since I was thrown out
Of the Garden of Eden.

But back to the poem.

Strange as it might seem
The psychiatrist was right
As he starts into a tunnel
The artist becomes delirious.
To begin with he's taken to a factory
There is where madness begins.

The principal symptom:
He relates everything to the act
He can't tell the sun from the moon
He relates everything to the act
Pistons are sex organs
Cylinders are sex organs
Turntables are sex organs
Crankshafts are sex organs
Blast furnaces are sex organs
Nuts and bolts are sex organs
Locomotives are sex organs
Ocean liners are sex organs.

There's no way out of the maze.

The West is a great pyramid
That ends and begins with a psychiatrist:
The pyramid is starting to crumble.

PARA QUE VEAS QUE NO TE GUARDO RENCOR

te regalo la luna
seriamente—no creas que me estoy burlando de ti:
te la regalo con todo cariño
¡nada de puñaladas por la espalda!
tú misma puedes pasar a buscarla
tu tío que te quiere
tu mariposa de varios colores
Directamente desde el Santo Sepulcro.

¡CUANTAS VECES VOY A REPETIR LO MISMO!

Compren insecticida
Saquen las telarañas del techo
Limpien los vidrios de las ventanas
¡están plagados de cagarrutas de moscas
Eliminen el polvo de los muebles
Y lo más urgente de todo:
háganme desaparecer las palomas:
¡todos los días me ensucian el auto!

¡Dónde demonios me dejaron los fósforos!

SO YOU CAN SEE I DON'T CARRY A GRUDGE

I give you the moon
Seriously—don't think I'm making fun of you:
I present it to you with the very deepest affection:
I'm not trying to pull anything!
you can go pick it up yourself
your uncle who loves you
your many-colored butterfly
Coming to you direct from the holy sepulcher.

HOW MANY TIMES DO I HAVE TO TELL YOU

Get some insecticide
Get the spider web off the ceiling
Wash the windows
They're covered with fly specks.
Dust the furniture
And most important of all:
get rid of these pigeons:
They're all the time messing on my car!

Where the devil did you leave the matches!

IDEAS SUELTAS

No me gusta mirarme
En los espejos salpicados de sangre.

Preferible dormir al aire libre
Antes que compartir
El lecho de bodas con una tortuga.

El automóvil es una silla de ruedas.

Y el infeliz que mira a la madre
En el momento mismo del parto
Queda marcado para sécula seculorum.

SHUFFLED THOUGHTS

I don't want to see myself
In blood-spattered mirrors.

I would rather sleep in the open
Than share
A marriage bed with a turtle.

The automobile is a wheelchair.

And the poor devil who looks at his mother
At the very moment of birth
Is marked forever
per secula seculorum.

LOS LIMITES DE CHILE

No es Chile el que limita con la Cordillera de los Andes, con el Desierto del Salitre, con el Océano Pacífico, con la unión de los dos océanos: la cosa es al revés. Es la Cordillera de los Andes la que limita con Chile, el Océano Pacífico es el que llega hasta la cumbre del Aconcagua. Son los 2 Océanos los que rompen en mil pedazos la monotonía del paísaje sureño. El río Valdivia es el lago más largo de Chile. Chile limita al Norte con el Cuerpo de Bomberos, al Sur con el Ministerio de Educación, al Este con la Cordillera de Nahuelbuta y al Oeste con el vacío que producen las olas del Océano que se nombró más arriba, al Sur con González Videla. En el medio hay una gran plasta rodeada de militares, curas y normalistas que suecunan (1) a través de cañerías de cobre.

(1) succionan.

THE BORDERS OF CHILE

It's not true that Chile is bordered by the Andes,
by the Saltpeter Desert, by the Pacific Ocean, by
the meeting of two oceans: it's just the opposite.
It's the Andes that are bordered by Chile, it's the
Pacific that reaches the rim of Aconcagua. (1)
It's the 2 oceans that break the monotony of the south country
into a thousand pieces. The Valdivia River
is the longest lake in Chile. Chile is bordered on the
North by the Fire Brigade, on the South by the Education
Department, on the East by the Nahuelbuta Range, and
on the West by the emptiness that makes the waves
of the Ocean named above, on the South by González
Videla. (2) In the middle is a great cowpile
surrounded by soldiers, priests and education
majors who souken (3) it up through copper water pipes.

(1) The largest volcano in Chile.
(2) An ex-president of Chile. Elected by the left, he turned against them once he was in office and forced a number of leaders of the left—including Neruda—into exile.
(3) suck.

LA BATALLA CAMPAL

la cosa comienza con un
DESFILE NOCTURNO DE ENERGUMENOS
por el centro de la ciudad:

¡ muerte sí!
¡ funerales nó!

¡ muerte sí!
¡ funerales nó!

¡ muerte sí!
¡ funerales nó!

LOS ROBBOTS OBSERVAN EL DESFILE DESDE SUS
CARROS DE COMBATE

y continúa al día siguiente
A LA HORA DE MAYOR TRAFICO
—entre 1 y 2 de la tarde—
BAJO UN SOL ABRASADOR
con una
MANIFESTACION PACIFICA DE ENERGUMENOS
envueltos en sábanas—con antorchas y cucuruchos
FRENTE A UNA TIENDA DE POMPAS FUNEBRES.
En teoría no molestan a nadie
y de hecho no hacen otra cosa
que cantar y bailar en tiempo de cumbia
DOS FRASES QUE REPITEN HASTA EL INFINITO

¡ muerte sí!
¡ funerales nó!

THE LAST BATTLE

the whole thing begins with a
NIGHT MARCH OF ENERGUMENS
through the center of the city:

death sí!
funerals no!

death sí!
funerals no!

death sí!
funerals no!

THE ROBOTS OBSERVE THE MARCH FROM THEIR
ARMORED CARS

and it goes on the next day
RIGHT AT RUSH HOUR
—between 1 and 2 in the afternoon—
UNDER A BOILING SUN
with a
PEACEFUL ENERGUMEN DEMONSTRATION
wrapped up in sheets—with torches and hoods.
IN FRONT OF A FUNERAL PARLOR.
in theory they don't bother anybody
in fact they do nothing
but sing and dance to a cumbia beat (1)

THEY REPEAT THESE TWO SLOGANS OVER AND OVER

death sí!
funerals no!

¡muerte sí!
¡funerales nó!

¡muerte sí!
¡funerales nó!

PERO LOS ROBBOTS OBSERVAN ATENTAMENTE
LOS ACONTECIMIENTOS DESDE SUS CARROS
DE COMBATE

al tercer día

LOS ENERGUMENOS
SE DIRIGEN TRANQUILAMENTE A SUS CASAS

después de varias horas de baile desenfrenado
FRENTE A LA MONEDA
cuando aparecen en escena los robbots
y comienza la batalla campal
Y COMIENZA LA BATALLA CAMPAL
¡Y COMIENZA LA BATALLA CAMPAL!

death sí!
funerals no!

death sí!
funerals no!

BUT THE ROBOTS OBSERVE EVERYTHING CLOSELY
FROM THEIR ARMORED CARS

on the third day
THE ENERGUMENS HEAD PEACEFULLY FOR HOME
after hours of nonstop dancing
IN FRONT OF THE WHITE HOUSE
when the robots come on the scene
and the last battle begins
AND THE LAST BATTLE BEGINS
AND THE LAST BATTLE BEGINS!

(1) A Latin dance with a strong and distinct rhythm.

MANIFIESTO

Señoras y señores
Esta es nuestra última palabra.
—Nuestra primera y última palabra—
Los poetas bajaron del Olimpo.

Para nuestros mayores
La poesía fue un objeto de lujo
Pero para nosotros
Es un artículo de primera necesidad:
No podemos vivir sin poesía.

A diferencia de nuestros mayores
—Y esto lo digo con todo respeto—
Nosotros sostenemos
Que el poeta no es un alquimista
El poeta es un hombre como todos
Un albañil que construye su muro:
Un constructor de puertas y ventanas.

Nosotros conversamos
En el lenguaje de todos los días
No creemos en signos cabalísticos.

Además una cosa:
El poeta está ahí
Para que el árbol no crezca torcido.

Este es nuestro mensaje.
Nosotros denunciamos al poeta demiurgo
Al Poeta Barata
Al poeta ratón de biblioteca.

MANIFESTO

Ladies and gentlemen
This is our final word
—Our first and final word—
The poets have come down from Olympus.

For the old folks
Poetry was a luxury item
But for us
It's an absolute necessity
We couldn't live without poetry.

Unlike our elders
—And I say it with all respect—
We maintain this
A poet is no alchemist
A poet is a man like all men
A bricklayer building his wall:
A maker of windows and doors.

We talk
With everyday words
We don't believe in cabalistic signs.

And one thing more:
The poet is there
To see to it the tree does not grow crooked.

This is our message.
We denounce the godlike poet
The Cockroach poet
The bookworm poet.

Todos estos señores
—Y esto lo digo con mucho respeto—
Deben ser procesados y juzgados
Por construir castillos en el aire
Por malgastar el espacio y el tiempo
Redactando sonetos a la luna
Por agrupar palabras al azar
A la última moda de París.
Para nosotros no:
El pensamiento no nace en la boca
Nace en el corazón del corazón.

Nosotros repudiamos
La poesía de gafas obscuras
La poesía de capa y espada
La poesía de sombrero alón.
Propiciamos en cambio
La poesía a ojo desnudo
La poesía a pecho descubierto
La poesía a cabeza desnuda.

No creemos en ninfas ni tritones.
La poesía tiene que ser esto:
Una muchacha rodeada de espigas
O no ser absolutamente nada.

Ahora bien, en el plano político
Ellos, nuestros abuelos inmediatos,
¡Nuestros buenos abuelos inmediatos!
Se refractaron y se dispersaron
Al pasar por el prisma de cristal.
Unos pocos se hicieron comunistas.
Yo no sé si lo fueron realmente.
Supongamos que fueron comunistas,
Lo que sé es una cosa:
Que no fueron poetas populares,
Fueron unos reverendos poetas burgueses.

All of these gentlemen
—And I say it with great respect—
Must be arraigned and tried
For building castles in the air
For wasting time and space
By composing sonnets to the moon
For putting words together by chance
Following the latest Paris fashion.
That's not for us!
A thought is not born in the mouth
It is born in the heart.

We repudiate
The poetry of dark glasses
The poetry of the cape and sword
The poetry of the plumed hat
We propose instead
The poetry of the naked eye
The poetry of the hairy chest
The poetry of the bare head.

We don't believe in nymphs or tritons.
Poetry has to be this:
A girl in a wheatfield—
Or it's absolutely nothing.

Well now, on the political level
They, our immediate forebears,
Our good immediate ancestors,
Refracted themselves, dispersed themselves
Passing through crystal prisms.
A few came out communists.
I don't know if they actually were.
Let's assume they were communists.
All I know is this:
They were not poets of the people
They were nothing but touted bourgeois poets

Hay que decir las cosas como son:
Sólo uno que otro
Supo llegar al corazón del pueblo.
Cada vez que pudieron
Se declararon de palabra y de hecho
Contra la poesía dirigida
Contra la poesía del presente
Contra la poesía proletaria.

Aceptemos que fueron comunistas
Pero la poesía fue un desastre
Surrealismo de segunda mano
Decadentismo de tercera mano,
Tablas viejas devueltas por el mar.
Poesía adjetiva
Poesía nasal y gutural
Poesía arbitraria
Poesía copiada de los libros
Poesía basada
En la revolución de la palabra
En circunstancias de que debe fundarse
En la revolución de las ideas.
Poesía de círculo vicioso
Para media docena de elegidos:
"Libertad absoluta de expresión."

Hoy nos hacemos cruces preguntando
Para qué escribirían esas cosas
¿Para asustar al pequeño burgués?
¡Tiempo perdido miserablemente!
El pequeño burgués no reacciona
Sino cuando se trata del estómago.

¡Qué lo van a asustar con poesías!

Let's face it:
Only one or two
Ever found a place
In the hearts of the people.
Whenever they could
They declared themselves by word and by deed
Against the poetry of purpose
Against the poetry of the present
Against the poetry of the proletariat.

Let's say they were communists
But the poetry was a disaster
Second-hand surrealism
Third-hand decadence
Old planks washed up by the sea.
Adjective poetry
Nasal and guttural poetry
Arbitrary poetry
Poetry copied from books
Poetry based on the revolution of words
—But in fact
Poetry must spring from the revolution of ideas—
Poetry of the endless circle
For half a dozen chosen people:
"Absolute freedom of expression."

Today we scratch our heads and wonder
Why would they write such stuff
To frighten the petit bourgeois?
What a waste of time!
The petit bourgeois won't react
unless his stomach is at stake.

After all who's afraid of poetry!

La situación es ésta:
Mientras ellos estaban
Por una poesía del crepúsculo
Por una poesía de la noche
Nosotros propugnamos
La poesía del amanecer.
Este es nuestro mensaje,
Los resplandores de la poesía
Deben llegar a todos por igual
La poesía alcanza para todos.

Nada más, compañeros
Nosotros condenamos
—Y esto sí que lo digo con respeto—
La poesía de pequeño dios
La poesía de vaca sagrada
La poesía de toro furioso.

Contra la poesía de las nubes
Nosotros oponemos
La poesía de la tierra firme
—Cabeza fría, corazón caliente
Somos tierrafirmistas decididos—
Contra la poesía de café
La poesía de la naturaleza
Contra la poesía de salón
La poesía de la plaza pública
La poesía de protesta social.

Los poetas bajaron del Olimpo.

Here's the situation:
They were for
Twilight poetry
Midnight poetry
We stand for
The poetry of dawn.
Our message is this:
The lights of poetry
Belong to everyone
Poetry takes care of us all.

That's it, comrades
We condemn
—And I'm not putting you on—
The poetry of the petty gods
The poetry of the sacred cow
The poetry of the angry bull.

Against
The poetry of the clouds
We set the poetry of terra firma
—cold hand, warm heart
We are decidedly terra firmers—
Against café poetry we set
The poetry of the open air
Against drawing room poetry—
The poetry of the public square
The poetry of social protest.

The poets have come down from Olympus.

DESCORCHO OTRA BOTELLA

y prosigo mi baile de costumbre

estiro una pierna
que perfectamente podría ser brazo
recojo un brazo
que perfectamente podría ser pierna

me encuclillo sin dejar de danzar
y me desabrocho los señores zapatos
uno lo lanzo más arriba del cielo
otro lo hundo hondo en la tierra

ahora comienzo a sacarme el sweater

en esto oigo sonar el teléfono
me llaman de la señora oficina
contesto que seguiré bailando
hasta que me suban el sueldo.

I UNCORK ANOTHER BOTTLE

and go into my usual dance

I stretch a leg
it could just as well be an arm
I fold an arm
it could just as well be a leg

I squat without stopping my dance
unbuckle both Mister Shoes
throw one of them higher than heaven
bury the other deep in the earth

I start to get out of my sweater

at this moment the telephone rings
they call me from Mrs. Office
I'm going to keep dancing I tell them
until they give me a raise

ALGUIEN DETRAS DE MI

lee cada palabra que escribo
por encima de mi hombro derecho
y se ríe desvergonzadamente de mis problemas
un señor de bastón y levita

miro pero no veo que haya nadie
sin embargo yo sé que me espían

SOMEBODY BEHIND ME

reads every word I write
looking over my left shoulder
he laughs at my problems with no shame
a man with a swagger stick and tails

I look but there's nobody there
still I know someone is watching me

YO JEHOVA DECRETO

que se termine todo de una vez
hago la cruz al sistema solar

hay que volver al útero materno
doy por finiquitada la cosa

que no se escape nadie
que se termine todo de golpe
para qué vamos a andar con rodeos

está muy bien   la Guerra de Viet-Nam
está muy bien   la Operación a la próstata
yo Jehová decreto la vejez

ustedes me dan risa
ustedes me ponen los nervios de punta
sólo un cretino de nacimiento
se arrodilla a venerar una estatua

francamente no sé que decirles
estamos al borde de la Tercera Guerra Mundial
y nadie parece darse cuenta de nada

si destruyen el mundo
¿creen que yo voy a volver a crearlo?

I JEHOVAH DECREE

that everything stop once and for all
I've had it with the solar system

we have to get back to the womb
and that's final

that nobody escape
bankruptcy: everything goes
there's no reason to horse around

that's just fine   the war in Vietnam
that's just fine   the prostate operation
I Jehovah decree old age

you make me laugh
you make my skin crawl
only a congenital idiot
kneels down to worship a statue

to tell you the truth I don't know what to say
we're standing on the brink of World War Three
and nobody seems tc give a damn for anything

if you destroy the world
do you think I'm going to create it all over again?

YO PECADOR

Yo galán imperfecto
Yo danzarín al borde del abismo,

Yo sacristán obsceno
Niño prodigio de los basurales,

Yo sobrino—yo nieto
Yo confabulador de siete suelas,

Yo señor de las moscas
Yo descuartizador de golondrinas,

Yo jugador de fútbol
Yo nadador del Estero las Toscas,

Yo violador de tumbas
Yo satanás enfermo de paperas,

Yo conscripto remiso
Yo ciudadano con derecho a voto,

Yo ovejero del diablo
Yo boxeador vencido por mi sombra,

Yo bebedor insigne
Yo sacerdote de la buena mesa,

Yo campeón de cueca
Yo campeón absoluto de tango
De guaracha, de rumba, de vals,

Yo pastor protestante
Yo camarón, yo padre de familia,

I, SINNER

I, imperfect gentleman
I Nijinsky at the edge of the abyss,

I, obscene sexton
Child prodigy of the garbage pile,

I, nephew—I, grandchild
I, totally untrustworthy schemer,

I, Lord of the Flies
I, mangler of swallows,

I, fútbol player
I, swimmer of the Estero las Toscas, (1)

I, violator of Tombs
I, Satan, afflicted with goiter,

I, draft dodger
I, citizen with the right to vote,

I, shepherd of Hell
I, boxer beaten by his own shadow,

I, illustrious drinker
I, priest of the laden table,

I, champion of the cueca (2)
I, undisputed champion of the tango
The huarache, the rhumba, the waltz,

I, protestant preacher
I, shrimp, I head of the family,

Yo pequeño burgués
Yo profesor de ciencias ocultas,

Yo comunista, yo conservador
Yo recopilador de santos viejos,

(Yo turista de lujo)

Yo ladrón de gallinas
Yo danzarín inmóvil en el aire,

Yo verdugo sin máscara
Yo semidiós egipcio con cabeza de pájaro,

Yo de pie en una roca de cartón:
Háganse las tinieblas
Hágase el caos,
                    háganse las nubes,

Yo delincuente nato
Sorprendido infraganti
Robando flores a la luz de la luna
Pido perdón a diestra y siniestra
Pero no me declaro culpable.

I, petit bourgeois
I, professor of occult sciences,

I, communist, I conservative
I, collector of old icons,

(I, V.I.P. tourist)

I, chicken thief
I, Nijinsky, hovering,

I, hangman with no hood
I, Egyptian demigod with a bird's head,

I, standing on a cardboard rock:
Let there be darkness
Let there be chaos,
let there be clouds,

I, congenital delinquent
Caught in the act
Stealing flowers by moonlight,
Beg you, Cowboys and Indians alike,
To forgive me
But I do not plead guilty.

(1) A small, dirty river—a sewer—in the city of Chillán in southern Chile.
(2) A dance done by a couple in a flirtatious fashion; often called the national dance of Chile.

ANTES ME PARECIA TODO BIEN

ahora todo me parece mal

un teléfono viejo de campanilla
bastaba para hacerme el sujeto más feliz de la creación
un sillón de madera-cualquier cosa

los domingos por la mañana
me iba al mercado persa
y regresaba con un reloj de pared
—es decir con la caja del reloj—
y las correspondientes telarañas
o con una Victrola desvencijada
a mi cabañísima de la Reina
donde me esperaba el Chamaco
y su señora madre de aquel entonces

eran días felices
o por lo menos noches sin dolor

EVERYTHING SEEMED FINE BEFORE

now everything seems awful

an old crank telephone
used to be all it took
to make me the happiest person in the world
or a wooden bench—anything—

sunday mornings
I used to go to the thieves' market
and come back with a wall clock
—that is to say the frame that held the clock—
and all the spider webs that came with it
or a brokendown Victrola
to my little hut in la Reina
where my Chamaco waited for me
with his mother of that time

those were happy days
the nights at least were painless

HASTA LUEGO

Ha llegado la hora de retirarse
Estoy agradecido de todos
Tanto de los amigos complacientes
Como de los enemigos frenéticos.
¡ Inolvidables personajes sagrados!
Miserable de mí
Si no hubiera logrado granjearme
La antipatía casi general:
¡ Salve perros felices
Que salieron a ladrarme al camino!
Me despido de ustedes
Con la mayor alegría del mundo.

Gracias, de nuevo, gracias
Reconozco que se me caen las lágrimas
Volveremos a vernos
En el mar, en la tierra donde sea.
Pórtense bien, escriban
Sigan haciendo pan
Continúen tejiendo telarañas
Les deseo toda clase de parabienes:
Entre los cucuruchos
De esos árboles que llamamos cipreses
Los espero con dientes y muelas.

HASTA LUEGO

The time has come to leave
I am grateful to all—
As much as for my complacent friends
As my frenetic enemies.
Those unforgettable holy creatures!
Hell
What if I hadn't earned
Almost universal antipathy!
God bless you happy dogs
Running out to bark at me on the road!
I bid you good-by
With the greatest joy in the world.

Thanks, and thanks again
Of course I'm crying
We'll meet again sometime,
On the sea, in some land or other.
Take care of yourselves, drop me a line
Go on baking bread
Keep on knitting spider webs
I wish you health wealth
And time to enjoy them
Among the dunce caps
Of these trees called cypresses
I wait with bared teeth.

UN SUJETO DE MALOS ANTECEDENTES

se desplaza por un laberinto
desde luego parece un insecto

habla hasta por los codos
se le sueltan las cuerdas vocales

cada vez más arrugas en la frente

masturbación a falta de suicidio

se queda con una bufanda prestada
no revisa las pruebas escritas
califica al azar a sus alumnos
hasta que lo sorprenden infraganti

circuncisión a los cincuenta años de edad
estornuda y escupe en el pañuelo
gesticula como un condenado
traductor de obras científicas
se divorcia
se casa nuevamente
deja de masturbarse por un tiempo
sensación de que alguien lo espía
agorafobia claustrofobia
pérdida del sentido del olfato
sueños apocalípticos
abre los brazos en señal de derrota.

A SUSPICIOUS CHARACTER

walks in a labyrinth
to begin with he looks like an insect

he talks and talks and talks
till his vocal cords come loose

his brow grows more and more wrinkled

masturbation instead of suicide

he keeps a borrowed scarf
he doesn't read exams
and grades his students by lot
till they catch him at it

circumcision at fifty
he sneezes and spits in his handkerchief
he gestures wildly
a translator of scientific works
is divorced
                gets married again
stops masturbating for a while
the fear that someone is watching
agoraphobia   claustrophobia
loses his sense of smell
dreams   apocalypses
he opens his arms   a sign of total defeat

EL HOMBRE CONTEMPORANEO

cayó en una trampa
sólo le quedan siete caminos
ninguno de los cuales conduce a Roma

SIETE

son los temas fundamentales de la poesía lírica
en primer lugar el pubis de la doncella
luego la luna llena que es el pubis del cielo
los bosquecillos abarrotados de pájaros
el crepúsculo que parece una tarjeta postal
el instrumento músico llamado violín
y la maravilla absoluta que es un racimo de uvas.

MODERN MAN

has fallen into a trap
he has only seven roads left
and none of them leads to Rome

SEVEN

the basic themes of lyric poetry are seven
the first one is the pubis of a maiden
then the full moon the pubis of the sky
a small stand of trees bowed down with birds
a sunset like a picture post card
the musical instrument they call a violin
and the absolute marvel of a bunch of grapes.

FELICITACIONES

y para terminar
felicito do todo corazón a S.E. el Presidente de la República
por su brillante Mensaje Presidencial

que el Espíritu Santo lo cubra de gracia
que la Virgen María lo bendiga
en compañía de señora y familia

que sus manos besa

felicito también a los señores bomberos
honra y prez de nuestra colectividad

se les saluda con la mayor devoción

doy las gracias al Supremo Hacedor
en el auspicioso día de su onomástico
que la Divina Providencia lo colme de gloria
su afmo y seguro servidor

que sus manos besa

felicito al Cuerpo Diplomático
por la colaboración prestada
a la prensa—a la radio—a la televisión
por la colaboración prestada

que sus manos besa

agradezco muy en particular
a los señores fotógrafos
ellos son nuestros terceros padres
a los periodistas desinteresados
ellos son nuestros padres ubérrimos

que sus manos besa

CONGRATULATIONS

and in closing
my heartiest congratulations to his Excellency the President
of the Republic
for his brilliant presidential address

may the Holy Spirit fill him with grace
may the Virgin Mary bless him
and his family also

A. M. D. G. (1)

congratulations also to the fire department
they are the pride and glory of our community

I salute you with the deepest devotion

all praise to the Most High Maker
on this auspicious day of his anniversary
may Divine Providence annoint him with glory
your most obedient and affectionate servant

A. M. D. G.

Congratulations to the Diplomatic Corps
for their most gracious help
to the press and radio and television
for their most gracious help

A. M. D. G.

I particularly appreciate
the distinguished photographers
our third fathers
the distinguished journalists
our most exalted fathers

A. M. D. G.

y volviendo a los señores fotógrafos
ellos saben fijar un instante de dicha
un bautizo—una boda—lo que sea
por eso digo que son nuestros terceros padres

que sus manos besa

felicito de todo corazón al Episcopado
y por qué no decirlo
felicito también a las Fuerzas Armadas
a los señores cosmonautas
a nuestros Hermanos de la Gran República del Norte
que exponiendo sus vidas personales
en beneficio de la Humanidad
ponen en jaque a los revoltosos
sin ambiciones de ninguna especie
animados por ese espíritu de sacrificio
de que sólo pueden hacer gala los espíritus superiores

doy las gracias al Supremo Hacedor
por haberme devuelto la salud
uno que está a las puertas de la muerte
pero la magnanimidad del Todopoderoso
me devolvió la vista

por la libre determinación de los pueblos
por un mundo sin explotadores
el orden público está asegurado

ése es el canto del cisne del capitalismo

el orden público está asegurado
nadie podrá romperlo nuevamente
sin exponer sus seguridad personal
honor y prez de nuestra institución

bendigo a la flor y nata de la intelectualidad chilena
que sus manos besa

getting back to our distinguished photographers
they know how to capture a joyous instant
a baptism—a wedding—anything at all
it is for this I call them our third fathers

A. M. D. G.

most hearty congratulations to all the bishops
and since I haven't said anything about them
congratulations also to the Armed Forces
also to the worthy cosmonauts
also our Brothers of the Grand Republic to the North
who at the risk of their lives
for the good of mankind
are putting the rebels in their place
motivated by no ambition at all
only by the spirit of sacrifice
which only goes to show their superior souls

thanks to the Most High Maker
for having returned me to health
I lay at death's door
but the magnanimity of His Omnipotence
restored my sight

for self-determination of the people
for a world without exploitation
Law and Order is being maintained

that's the swan song of capitalism

Law and Order is being maintained
nobody can break it ever again
without putting his life on the line
honor and glory to our institution

blessings on the flower and the cream
of our Chilean intelligentsia

A. M. D. G.

gloria a sus ex-alumnos distinguidos
gloria a sus esforzados inspectores
y que el Señor los colme de beneficios
ellos son nuestros terceros padres

no se trata de amenazar a nadie
ésta es una simple advertencia
declararé feriado nacional

felicito de todo corazón a los oradores
que me han precedido en el uso de la palabra
al señor Rector del Liceo de Hombres
a la señorita Marta Brunet Premio Nacional de Literatura
que tuvo la amabilidad de dirigirnos la palabra
al Director del Diario la Discusión
al Director Interino de Impuestos Internos
a la Madre Superiora de la Casa Correcional
a los detectives caídos en cumplimiento del deber
un capitán en acto de servicio

un capitán de ejército
vale más que un profesor de literatura
un coronel en acto de servicio
vale más que todas la obras de arte de los museos

felicito de todo corazón
a los Ancianos del Instituto de Recuperación
a la Gota de Leche
a los pacientes del Instituto Pedagógico
por el método de asociación de ideas

ustedes están asistiendo a los funerales del yo poético
que reventó por exceso de delicadeza

a depositar una corona de rosas
en la tumba del poeta desconocido

glory be to its distinguished former students
glory to its well-intentioned inspectors
may the Lord annoint them with benefactions
these are our third fathers

nobody's trying to threaten anybody
this is a simple warning
I will declare a judicial holiday

heartiest congratulations to the public speakers
whose rhetoric preceded mine
and the distinguished principal of the School for Boys
and Miss Martha Brunet, winner of the National Prize
for Literature,
who was kind enough to share a few words with us
and to the Editor of The Daily Discussion
the Director pro tem of Internal Revenue
the Mother Superior of the Correctional Home
and to all the detectives who fell in the line of duty
a captain on active duty

an army captain
is worth more than any professor of literature
a colonel on active duty
is worth more than all the art in all the museums

congratulations from the bottom of my heart—
to all the Old Folks in the Nursing Home
to the Salvation Army
to those patients at the University of Chile—
through the association of ideas

now you are attending the Funeral of The Muse
who exploded from too much delicacy

lay a wreath of roses
on the tomb of the unknown poet

(1) *Ad Mejorem Dei Gloriam.* Literally, "To the Greater Glory of God."

CANCION PARA CORRER EL SOMBRERO

En su granja de Iásmaia Poliana
vivió muchos años el Conde Leof Nicolaievich Tolstoy
no se afeitaba jamás—andaba siempre descalzo
Dios lo tenga en su santo reino
Sólo comía zanahorias crudas

Ustedes se preguntarán quién soy yo
con esta barba blanca tolstoiana
pidiendo limosna en la vía pública
ay!... yo soy uno de sus nietos legítimos

La Revolución ha sido dura conmigo
para qué voy a decir una cosa por otra
que cada cual me dé lo que pueda
(aquí se empieza a correr el sombrero)
todo me sirve aunque sea un kopek

Ay!... si yo les contara todos mis sufrimientos
imaginen el nieto de un Conde
pidiendo limosna en la vía pública:
¡Es para poner los pelos de punta!

Además mi mujer se fue con otro
me dejó por un capitán de ejército
so pretexto de que soy paralítico
no negaré que soy paralítico
—¡tiemblo como una hoja en la tormenta!—
pero me parece que no se puede romper
un sacramento de la Santa Madre Iglesia Católica
como quien rompe globos de colores:
hay señoras mujeres en el siglo XX
que se debieran desmayar de vergüenza

Ay ay ay—ay ay ay—ay ay aycito
compadézcanse de este pobre cornudo
no dispongo de otra fuente de ingresos.

SONG TO PASS AROUND THE HAT*

For years Count Leo Nikolaievich Tolstoy
lived on his estate in Iasmaia Poliana
he never shaved—and went around barefoot
may he have a place in heaven
he ate only raw carrots

No doubt you're asking yourselves who I am
with this white Tolstoyan beard
begging money in a public street
I—I one of his legitimate grandchildren

The Revolution has been cruel to me
I'm not going to say one thing and mean another
but if each of you could give whatever you can—
(Here he passes the hat around)
anything will do—even a single kopeck

I . . . if only I could tell you all my sufferings
imagine! the grandson of a Count
begging in a public street:
It stands your hair on end!

My wife furthermore ran away with another man
she left me for an army captain
on the pretext that I had a nervous disorder
I won't deny that I quake all over
as a matter of fact
I tremble like a leaf in a storm!
but it seems to me you don't break
a sacrament of Our Holy Mother Church
the way you pop party balloons:
there are some respectable twentieth-century ladies
who ought to faint from shame

I . . . yi yi—I . . . yi yi—*I yi yi*
pity this poor cuckold
who hasn't any other source of income

Para qué voy a decir una cosa por otra
sufro de una enfermedad incurable
contraída en la más tierna infancia:
tengo todo el lado derecho paralizado
me puedo morir en cualquier momento

Mi enfermedad se llama encefalitis letárgica.

Para colmo de males
acaban de operarme de la vesícula
si les parece les muestro la cicatriz.

Ay!... no tengo paz en ninguna parte
para qué voy a decir una cosa por otra
los pelusas del barrio me persiguen tirándome piedras
hay que ser bien caído del catre
para reirse de un pobre viejo zarrapastroso
que no tiene ni donde caerse muerto
Si mi querido abuelo estuviera vivo
yo no tendría que andar pidiendo limosna
¡otro gallo muy diferente me cantaría!

Dicho sea de paso tengo que juntar 17 dólares
antes que me venga el ataque
para pagar mi dosis de heroína
a buen entendedor pocas palabras
si no me dan por la buena
van a tener que darme por la mala
para qué vamos a decir una cosa por otra
yo soy bien hombrecito en mis cosas
arriba las manos maricones de mierda
vamos saltando o les saco la chucha!

I'm not going to say one thing and mean another
I suffer from an incurable disease
contracted in my earliest childhood:
my entire right side quakes uncontrollably
I may die at any moment

My disease is encephalitis lethargica

On top of all this
I've just had vesicular surgery
if you want me to I'll show you the scar

I . . . I can't find peace anywhere
I'm not going to say one thing and mean another
the neighborhood kids are always after me, throwing stones
you really have to be sick
to make fun of a ragged old soul
who doesn't have a place to die
If my dear grandfather were only alive today
I wouldn't have to go around begging
a different bird would be singing my song!

By the way I've got to get 17 dollars
to pay for my heroin booster shot
before I have an attack
don't make me draw you a picture
if you don't give it to me
I'll have to get it myself
I'm not going to pull any punches
I'm a tough little bastard in my way
stick 'em up   your money or your ass
up against the wall motherfuckers!

* To be sung to a Gregorian chant.

INDEX OF SPANISH TITLES AND FIRST LINES

INDEX OF ENGLISH TITLES AND FIRST LINES